THE STORY OF
SAINT F…)
BISHOP OF (…

Prepared for the Dean and Chapter of Chichester by
Michael Gudgeon,
Priest-in-charge of the parish of St Andrew the Apostle, Worthing

Based on *The Life of Saint Richard* by
Friar Ralph Bocking and other ancient sources,
translated and edited by David Jones
and used with his permission.

PHOTO CREDITS
Unless otherwise stated, illustrations are from the Chichester Cathedral Library.
New photography commissioned for this book © Peter Smith: 11 (top and bottom), 17 (top and bottom), 23, 26 (top), 27, 28, 30, 31, back cover
© Peter Atkinson: 8 (top), 26 (far right);
© Brian Boucher, with permission of St Andrew's PCC: front cover, inside cover, 13, 25
© John Crook: 2
© Dean and Chapter of Westminster: 32
© Michael Gudgeon, with permission of the Vicar of St Mary's: 26 (left)
© Editions Gaud: 7
© Jeremy Haselock: 26 (bottom, right)
© Judges of Hastings: 8, 15, 16, 21
© Thomas Photos, Oxford: 5

SCALA

CHICHESTER CATHEDRAL

ST RICHARD WAS BORN IN DROITWICH IN 1197,
NSECRATED BISHOP OF CHICHESTER ON 5 MARCH
DIED AT DOVER ON 3 APRIL 1253,
AND CANONIZED ON 22 JANUARY 1262.
HIS BODY WAS TRANSLATED TO THE SHRINE IN
CHICHESTER CATHEDRAL ON 16 JUNE 1276.

INTRODUCTION

On 16 June 1276 Chichester was for a few hours the centre of England. King Edward I, Queen Eleanor, the Archbishop of Canterbury and other bishops, and a great crowd of people had come to honour St Richard. In the words of the pope's decree of canonization, Richard had been 'placed in the catalogue of saints'.

Richard had died twenty-three years earlier, on 3 April 1253. He had been Bishop of Chichester for just over eight years, but in that brief time had become so beloved of the people of Sussex that his tomb immediately became a place of pilgrimage and prayer.

This book is published to mark the 750th anniversary of St Richard's death, in the hope that all who read it may be moved to join the people of Sussex in thanking God for their patron saint and to follow his example of devotion to Jesus.

Michael Gudgeon

FATHER WE GIVE YOU THANKS
THAT YOUR GLORY IS REVEALED IN ST RICHARD.
IN HIS LIFE YOU HAVE GIVEN US
AN EXAMPLE OF FAITHFULNESS TO CHRIST.
IN HIS HOLINESS WE FIND
ENCOURAGEMENT AND HOPE.
IN OUR COMMUNION WITH HIM
WE SHARE THE UNITY OF YOUR KINGDOM.

From the Order of the Eucharist on St Richard's Day

THE STORY OF SAINT RICHARD

BISHOP OF CHICHESTER

RICHARD OF WYCH

Like other medieval clerics, Richard took his surname from the place of his birth, the Worcestershire town of Wych (now Droitwich). The old Anglo-Saxon word *wic*, meaning village or settlement, had come to be associated with salt works, and so it was the salt springs of Wych that gave the town its name. Born in about 1197, Richard was one of at least three children, including an elder brother. His parents, Richard and Alice, were of 'not ignoble status', according to Friar Ralph Bocking, the saint's confessor and biographer. They owned the land they farmed.

We are told that Richard 'applied himself from his youth to the study of letters'. This was not unusual for a younger son, who might expect to find his living as a clerk – that is an educated man, fit for service in church or state, but not necessarily a priest. Richard went to study in Oxford, but his studies were interrupted by problems at home. His father had died before he and his elder brother had come of age, and it seems that their guardian had mismanaged their inheritance.

On his return home to help his brother run the estate, Richard worked so generously and efficiently that his brother offered to give him both the property and the hand of the heiress to whom he was betrothed. But Richard's desire to study was more than the choice of a sensible career. He saw it as his calling from God and so, choosing 'an inheritance incorruptible and undefiled, reserved in heaven' (1 Peter 1:4), returned to his studies in Oxford.

Above: Wall mosaic in the Church of the Sacred Heart, Droitwich, depicting Richard ploughing on his family's farm. The entire nave is decorated with scenes from Richard's life.

RICHARD – STUDENT AND TEACHER

During the twelfth century, schools of study, often attached to cathedrals or monasteries, had gradually become independent universities. Among them Paris, Bologna and Oxford had attained this status by the time of Richard's birth, and Cambridge followed in 1209. The growing independence of Oxford from the Bishop of Lincoln was marked by the appointment of its own chancellor, first recorded in 1214.

At Oxford Richard followed the normal course of studies, and was awarded the degree of Master of Arts. He may also have studied in the universities of Paris, by now noted for theology, and Bologna, noted for canon law. Textbooks of canon law – church law as opposed to secular – were being copied and distributed throughout Europe, as the Church tried to bring order out of the many conflicting local codes of law. Richard certainly studied it in Oxford, being the earliest recorded Doctor of Canon Law in the university.

By now Richard was about forty and his academic standing was great enough for him to be chosen for the office of chancellor. This was not an honorary post as it is now, but the legal and administrative head of the university. It was perhaps Richard's holding of this office in the years 1235–37 that led the recently elected Archbishop of Canterbury, Edmund of Abingdon, to appoint him to his household

The Crypt of St Peter's Church, one of the buildings remaining from Oxford as it was in Richard's day. The church is now the library of St Edmund Hall, named after Richard's patron and perhaps standing on the site of his house.

ARCHBISHOP EDMUND

In 1231 Richard le Grand, Archbishop of Canterbury, had died after only three years in office. The monks of Canterbury found it hard to choose a successor who was acceptable to all concerned, and three elections were annulled. Eventually, in 1234, they elected the learned and saintly Edmund of Abingdon.

There was much to be done in a diocese that had been vacant for three years. To help him in his work of reform and renewal, Edmund appointed Richard as his chancellor. This position was a chief secretary with increasing legal authority. Richard was to be one of Edmund's closest supporters for the rest of his life, and after his death he became a leading advocate of Edmund's canonization. As Friar Ralph wrote, 'Each leaned upon the other – the saint upon the saint, the master upon the disciple, the disciple upon the master, the father on the son, the son on the father' (*Life*, Book 1, section 7).

In the England of Henry III, the Archbishop of Canterbury was bound to be caught up in affairs of state. As in the days of Henry II and Archbishop Thomas Becket, seventy years before, there were many opportunities for conflict between king and bishops. These potential sources of conflict included the differing rights of church courts and royal courts, and the practice of paying for royal and papal officials with the income of church offices such as canonries and deaneries. So, for example, the royal chancellor and treasurer were usually bishops, while the pope would often nominate one of his officials to be the priest of an English parish. In addition, the king claimed the income of vacant bishoprics and other offices. This inevitably led to friction between pope, king and archbishop for the right to appoint, as well as pressure on the monks or canons of a cathedral who had the right to elect the bishop. Even when relationships between church and state were tranquil, the king would claim the right to approve the appointment of archbishops and bishops, on the understandable grounds that they were powerful figures in the secular world as well as in the church.

For a few years Archbishop Edmund was able to lead the bishops in supporting the king, in arranging a truce with his enemies, and in a ratification of Magna Carta in 1238. This averted a civil war between the king and barons, but almost immediately Henry tried to strengthen his own hand by playing off the pope's legate, Cardinal Otto, against bishops as

CHURCH APPOINTMENTS

In earlier ages it was taken for granted that income from church appointments could be used to pay clerks who were doing other work. Bishops, popes and kings would therefore try to appoint their officials – and even their friends – to lucrative positions in the church. They would often leave a poorly paid deputy, or a legal representative, to do the work, while most of the income went to the absentee office holder.

It was only in the nineteenth century that the practices of absenteeism and pluralism (holding more than one church office) were tackled in the Church of England.

The Cistercian abbey church of Pontigny where Richard stayed with Archbishop Edmund in 1240.

well as barons. At the same time Edmund was having trouble with the monks of his own cathedral, who were opposing his attempts at reform. So, with his authority challenged by the king and his own cathedral, he set off for Rome in the autumn of 1240 to discuss his problems with Pope Gregory.

Like his predecessor St Thomas Becket, Edmund stayed at the abbey of Pontigny in northern Burgundy (now in the French Departement of Yonne). Accompanied by Richard, he lived there as a member of the strict Cistercian community. However, the political situation in Italy and his own poor health led him to abandon his journey to Rome. He died while returning to England, on 16 November 1240. As he had requested, his body was taken back to Pontigny.

SAINT EDMUND

Richard was one of the commissioners who collected evidence of miracles worked in England at Edmund's intercession. Six years after his death Edmund was canonized and his body was enshrined at Pontigny, where it still remains.

Throughout his life Richard sought to extend the honour paid to his master and friend. While studying in Orleans 'he built an oratory in honour of the blessed Edmund where he offered up to God celebrations of the mass and the holy outpourings of his prayers' (*Life*, Book 1, section 9). Richard's last act as a bishop, four days before his death in Dover, was to consecrate a chapel in honour of St Edmund. It was a cemetery chapel for the House of God (Maison Dieu), which stood

The chapel of St Edmund in Dover, dedicated by St Richard on 30 March 1253, four days before his death.

on the site of the present Town Hall and was a hospice run by a religious brotherhood to provide temporary lodgings for pilgrims and to care for the ill and the destitute. The chapel survived the Dissolution in the sixteenth century and is now restored to use.

AFTER THE DEATH OF EDMUND

After Edmund's death Richard went to Orleans to continue his studies in the house of the Friars Preacher (Dominicans), and there he was ordained priest, probably in 1243. It is known that he made a solemn promise to become a Dominican, and perhaps it was made at this time.

A new Archbishop of Canterbury was appointed in 1241 to succeed Richard's master. Boniface was a very different man from Edmund. Belonging to the family of the counts of Savoy, he was in fact the uncle of Queen Eleanor, wife of Henry III. He was heavily involved in the political life of Europe, and so did not arrive in England until 1244. This had left the archbishopric effectively vacant for four years. Boniface firmly allied himself with the reforming party in the Church.

The church of St Peter and St Paul, Charing, which honours Richard as a former parish priest.

THE CHURCH IN ST RICHARD'S TIME

The twelfth century had seen the growth of devotion to the humanity of Jesus, seeing him as saviour rather than as judge. In *The Twelfth-Century Renaissance*, Christopher Brooke describes him as 'the suffering Jesus ... the God-made man who lived in a particular part of the globe, which could be visited by adventurous pilgrims and recovered for Christendom by dedicated Crusaders'. Along with this devotion to the human Jesus went devotion to Mary, his human mother, which is expressed in the building of chapels and churches dedicated to her and in the increasing use of prayers such as the 'Hail Mary'. Friar Ralph Bocking's account of St Richard's death includes prayers to Jesus and to Mary.

This was also a time when new religious orders were being founded. Among Richard's contemporaries were Dominic (1170–1221), Francis of Assisi (1181–1226) and Clare (1193–1253).

Francis was the founder of the Friars Minor (commonly called Grey Friars from their habit). His devotion to the humanity of Jesus is shown both in his setting up of the first Christmas crib and by his receiving the *stigmata* – the marks of the Lord's wounds in hands, feet and side. The first group of Franciscans arrived in England in 1224, and there was a house in Chichester (where St Mary's Hospital now stands) before 1232.

Dominic was the founder of the Order of Preachers (Black Friars from their black cloaks). As their title implies they were specifically devoted to preaching and teaching, and played an important part in the development of universities throughout Europe. Friar Ralph, himself a Dominican, tells us that Richard 'bound himself to enter that excellent order of the Friars Preacher, and would have done so had it not been for the lord pope, who in approving the archbishop of Canterbury's decision to provide him to the diocese of Chichester, absolved him from that vow'.

Richard was a supporter of both Dominicans and Franciscans and in his will he left books and money to their houses in Chichester, Lewes, Winchelsea, Arundel, Canterbury and London.

Above: St Francis of Assisi (1181–1226), founder of the Friars Minor. 13th-century wall painting in the Benedictine monastery of Subiaco, Rome.

Left: St Dominic (1170–1221), founder of the Friars Preacher. From the Thornham Parva Retable, c.1336, originally made for the Dominican church at Thetford. It is now at St Mary's, Thornham Parva, Suffolk.

Boniface may have thought that Richard, as a disciple of archbishop Edmund and his martyred predecessor, St Thomas Becket, would be a useful ally in his work of reform. For whatever reason, he recalled Richard to the office of chancellor. Perhaps in connection with this office Richard was appointed to the parish of Charing, in the diocese of Canterbury. He also had responsibilities in Deal, but it is not clear what these were.

Meanwhile Ralph Neville, who was both Bishop of Chichester and Chancellor of England, had died. The king was no doubt anxious to keep the office and its revenue to support one of his ministers, so he would have been pleased when the canons of Chichester chose Robert Passelewe, one of the royal clerks, as their new bishop. Robert was already Archdeacon of Lewes and Prebendary of Marden. However, Boniface did not think him fit to be a bishop and, along with the other bishops of the province, refused to confirm the election. Instead the bishops chose the archbishop's nominee – his chancellor, Richard.

RICHARD BECOMES BISHOP OF CHICHESTER

King Henry was angry when he learned that his clerk had been replaced by Richard as bishop-elect of Chichester. He refused to return the temporalities (the property and income of the bishopric). Twice Richard approached the king in person, asking for royal confirmation of his election and the return of the episcopal estates, but on both occasions the king refused. Eventually both the king and Richard appealed to Pope Innocent IV, who was presiding over a church council in Lyons. The pope decided in favour of Richard and consecrated him as bishop on 5 March 1245.

Bishop Richard returned to England to find that the king still refused to hand over the estates. In fact he ordered that Richard should be kept out of all his houses, including the recently rebuilt palace at Chichester, and even forbade anyone to lend him money or give him shelter. It was to be two years before the king, threatened with excommunication by the pope, agreed to accept Richard as bishop and surrender the estates. Even then he did not restore the income of the previous two years, and at Richard's death it was still unpaid. Richard's will includes the following: 'I will also that … there be exacted from my Lord King by my executors the fruits of the bishopric of Chichester, which he for two years took unjustly and which of right belong to me, and payment of which I shall also seek in the Court of the Most High unless he has fully satisfied my executors'.

BISHOP RICHARD AT TARRING

So it was that Richard 'returned from the king a poor beggar and was received in his diocese like a traveller in a foreign land or, to be more precise, like someone taken in under another man's roof, placing his feet under a stranger's table and forced to learn, as the common phrase goes, to warm his feet by another man's fire'.

Friar Ralph continues:

> However, God often aids his servants in times of trouble and he provided Richard with a man after his own heart living not far from the seat of his diocese. This was Father Simon of Tarring – may his name live for ever and may his memory never fade! – whose virtuous life and reputation were well known, for he was filled more than other men with the bowels of Christ's love. God had touched this man's heart and he respectfully received the blessed Richard, whom he had already known in better days, as if the bishop were his own father, and placed at his disposal his house and everything which he owned. (*Life*, Book 1, section 14)

From Simon's home Richard 'did what good works he could, journeyed about his diocese, by turns visiting monasteries, offering counsel, and devoutly administering those sacraments which he saw to be needful'.

Above: Fig tree in the village of West Tarring. Friar Ralph describes Richard helping to graft trees in Simon's garden. A Sussex tradition tells that the fig trees for which Tarring became famous were planted by Richard. This is just one of many links made between the saint's farming background and his ministry as a bishop.

Right: The 13th-century palace of the archbishops of Canterbury in West Tarring, where Father Simon gave shelter to St Richard.

BISHOP RICHARD AND THE APOSTOLIC RULE

Friar Ralph based much of his life of St Richard on *The Apostolic Rule*. This was the medieval ideal of a bishop, drawn chiefly from two New Testament passages – the third chapter of the first letter to Timothy and the first chapter of the letter to Titus. Friar Ralph illustrates Richard's faithfulness to this model with examples of his temperance and prudence, his generous hospitality, his teaching, his patience under suffering, and the way he 'ruled his household'.

He writes of Richard: 'How nobly and how virtuously he lived his life and how prudently and carefully he ruled his church will be shown most clearly when his manner of life is compared to what is laid down by the Apostle. The first section of the Apostle's Rule is this: "a bishop must be blameless" [1 Timothy 3:2] or "without sin" [Titus 1:6], which comes to the same thing' (*Life*, Book 1, section 17).

Later he writes: 'God had so completely filled his heart with the virtue of hospitality that he would open the lap of his mercy to all who approached him and as far as possible receive them with honour under the roof of his earthly house ... for he was always careful to remember that saying of Our Lord which, as he himself bears witness, will be recalled at the Last Judgement: "I was a stranger and you took me in" [Matthew 25:35]'.

Ralph goes on to explain that a bishop's ruling of his household means the way he governs the different parts of his diocese:

> The household of a bishop is divided, as it were, into three parts and he must rule each of these well: first there is the clergy of his cathedral church, secondly there is his own household, and thirdly there is the population of the whole diocese under his authority.
>
> In the first of these areas the blessed Richard ruled as a master does his pupils, in the second as a father does his sons, in the third as a nurse does the infants in her care ... For it is the duty of the nurse to wash the child when he is dirty, to soothe him when he is distressed, to feed him when he is hungry. Thus did the blessed Richard cleanse the less sophisticated members of his flock as if they were small boys covered in dirt with the Word of his holy preaching, the tearful compunction of his holy prayers, the discipline of stern correction. (*Life*, Book 1, section 28)

RICHARD THE REFORMER

In 1215 Pope Innocent III had called the Fourth Lateran Council to further the reform of the Church. Innocent had a high view of papal authority, and was concerned to assert the freedom of the Church from secular control. This concern shows in the decrees of the council, but it was even more concerned to raise the standards of the parish

20th-century statue of St Richard in the church of St Andrew the Apostle, Worthing. He holds a model of Chichester Cathedral, and an overturned chalice lies at his feet (see page 25).

clergy, declaring that 'the government of souls is the art of arts'. It made rules about the education of the clergy and their moral discipline. It required them to refuse secular office, not to engage in trade and to avoid worldly pastimes. To make sure its decrees were effective, it ordered annual diocesan synods at which the bishop would instruct the clergy in their duties. In the words of notable historian Maurice Powicke, the council intended to provide 'a body of disciplined, educated clergy, armed with an orthodox creed against the heretical tendencies of the time and qualified, by character and training, to instruct their parishioners and to hear their confessions at least once a year' (*Oxford History of England: the Thirteenth Century*).

Richard – like his teacher Edmund – was one of the bishops who tried to apply this reform in England. His synodal statutes are the earliest known for the diocese of Chichester. He was concerned not only for the reverent celebration of the sacraments and the divine office, but for marriage discipline and the lifestyle of the clergy. He insisted that monasteries which had the care of parishes should appoint suitable vicars. In particular he forbade the appointment of laymen as vicars, and required that they should have stipends. He required rectors to live in their parishes 'as far as possible offering hospitality and carrying out other works of mercy'. He forbade any cleric to have a concubine, to engage in trade or secular administration, to dress as a layman or to hunt. He required the clergy to attend the diocesan synod, bringing with them notebooks in which to write his instructions.

But Richard was not concerned only for the clergy: 'We wish all the laity to attend divine service at least on Sunday and other holy days ... lest they cease to hear the divine office and their hearts become hardened. We also wish the laity to be urged by their priests to learn the Lord's Prayer and the Apostles' Creed and the Hail Mary, and parish priests should teach these, at least in the mother tongue, frequently and carefully' (Statute 70).

The list of those excommunicated by Richard's statutes show the range of a medieval bishop's involvement with the daily life of his people. They include lawyers who maliciously intervene in marriage cases, 'those who out of malice impede properly made wills, all fire-raisers, usurers, thieves, violators of church privileges' and 'those who for gain or out of hatred or favour or for whatever reason shall maliciously impute a fault to someone of good repute so that he is slandered' (Statutes 74, 75 and 76).

MIRACLES

Much of Friar Ralph's *Life* is taken up with descriptions of miracles, some performed by Richard during his lifetime, others in response to prayers invoking his assistance. Friar Ralph tells us that:

> even before he became bishop, he found at Orpington in Kent a boy who was paralysed and had lost the use of his limbs ... Struck with compassion for the unfortunate boy, he had him carried to his own house and, like the Samaritan, gave instructions that he should be cared for there ... When he had blessed him and with his own hands held out St Edmund's chalice for him to drink from it, the boy stood up and was restored to health. (*Life*, Book 1, section 30)

Many other miracles of healing are recorded, such as the restored eyesight of a noble lady, Alice; the cure of Maud, a paralysed laundress in Bignor; and of John Stokes, paralysed and suffering from terrible sores. A deaf man called Richard regains his hearing, another Richard, a boy dying at Lewes castle, is saved, and a nun named Helen has her toothache cured. There are also several accounts of the dead being restored to life, including this one set in the Wiltshire village of Winterbourne Earls sometime after Richard's death:

> This is what happened when the boy was nearly two years old. It was the feast of St Mary Magdalen [22 July] and ... the child had been rather carelessly left outside to play in the street. At about midday a carter suddenly drove his wagon up from the market place ... the horse crashed into the boy, who was knocked to the ground. As he lay there on his back the wheel of the cart ... drove over the boy's soft and tender stomach, killing the boy and shattering his body... The rector of the local church arrived. He could see that the boy was already shrouded in the pallor of death and that no signs of life remained in him ... While they were standing round the body the priest remembered a miracle which had been worked by the merits of the blessed Richard. Thus divinely inspired he said, 'Let us all kneel and humbly beg our Lord that at the intercession of the blessed Richard he may breathe life back into this dead child.' And to this end he told each of them to say three Our Fathers and three Hail Marys in honour of our Lord, our Lady and St Richard.
>
> The priest himself added several psalms and a prayer, but before the prayer was over the boy began to move first one foot, then the other and then, to the amazement of those present, he opened his eyes and let out a healthy laugh as a sign that not only had his life been restored to him, but he had been restored to full health. (*Life*, Book 2, section 11)

Friar Ralph also records how people were healed through contact with Richard's bed, hat or boots, just as in the Acts of the Apostles where healings were performed through cloths touched by St Paul.

Panel depicting the miracle of the fish, from a series embroidered for Chichester Cathedral in 1975 to commemorate the 900th anniversary of the Cathedral. Designed by Yvonne Hudson and Rosalie Williams.

As well as miracles of healing there are, as in the gospels, nature miracles including catches of fish, multiplication of food, the stilling of a storm, and this story of the re-lighting of a candle which was blown out during the Candlemas procession:

It was in Cakeham [one of the bishop's manors in the Selsey peninsular] that the 'true Light who enlightens everyone who comes into this world' showed how truly Blessed Richard belonged to the ranks of those to whom he said: 'You are the light of the world'. For when the saint himself was celebrating mass there on the feast of the Purification of the Blessed Virgin … the candles, which the bishop and all the others were holding according to custom, were blown out by a gust of wind. And when they had continued in the procession for some time using the candles that had been blown out, the others were suddenly astonished to see that the bishop's candle and it alone was alight again. When the bishop saw that his candle was lit once more he too was amazed and said to one of his attendants, 'Who lit my candle?' The attendant replied, 'No-one, my Lord'. The bishop said 'Hold your peace', and bade him not speak of the matter. For he did not wish to take for himself the light of vainglory from this miraculous light, as if repeating our Lord's saying 'I do not receive light from men'. O light, set up on the worthy candlestick of the Church, which defied the winds of popular favour and with a sincere heart aimed his own light at the Father of Lights!' (*Life*, Book 1, section 34)

BISHOP ODO ON MIRACLES

Bishop Odo presided over the inquiry that led to the canonization of St Richard. Here he speaks of the meaning of miracles performed by God at the intercession of the saints:

God is wonderful in his saints. Just as he made heaven and earth and the other visible and invisible things … so also does he work these miracles through the merits of his saints, in order that we may perceive his omnipotence, which performs such amazing and unaccustomed wonders outside and beyond and indeed contrary to nature; and so that his surpassing wisdom, which makes the impossible possible, should be revealed to us. Thus does the Lord show the wisdom of this world to be a foolish and empty thing, for he does things which man's skill cannot rival and which our understanding cannot grasp …

And, although he could do these things without the merits or intercession of the saints, he performs them through their merits and intercession to show how glorious it is to serve such a Lord, who rewards his servants in this fashion, and to draw us towards a mutual love by the means of the favours and graces he bestows upon us by and through his saints.

SAINT RICHARD'S CATHEDRAL

In 1075 the seat of the Sussex bishopric was moved from Selsey, where it had been established by St Wilfrid, to Chichester. A new cathedral was begun on the site of the minster church of St Peter. It was not until 3 October 1184 that the new church was consecrated, and just over three years later a serious fire destroyed much of its fabric as well as the Bishop's Palace and many other buildings in the city.

It was during the twelfth century that the style of building we call Gothic began in France, and it was spreading to England at about the time of Richard's birth. Following the fire of 1187, Chichester's Romanesque nave, with its round arches, was re-roofed in stone, and the retrochoir and western part of the Lady Chapel were rebuilt in the new Gothic style. Enough of the building was complete for a re-consecration on 12 September 1199, but the work of rebuilding and enlarging the cathedral went on throughout Richard's lifetime.

By the time he became bishop in 1245, Richard's cathedral had nave and aisles vaulted in stone, the north and south transepts with their chapels, the choir, the retrochoir with its chapels of St John the Baptist and St Mary Magdalen, and the Lady Chapel (shorter than it is now). There were north and south porches and three towers, but no spire.

The Bishop's Palace had been rebuilt after the fire and, although little from that date is now visible, the heart of the palace remains the beautiful thirteenth-century chapel, which Richard knew and used, and in which the bishop and his household still meet to worship and pray.

Detail from a carving of Christ raising Lazarus, in the south choir aisle of Chichester Cathedral. One of two panels which were probably part of the choir screen of the 11th-century building.

Church art at this time reflected the new devotion to the humanity of Jesus and Mary. At Chichester the majestic Christ of the carvings in the south aisle of the cathedral can be contrasted with the tender wall painting of the Virgin with her infant son in the chapel of the Bishop's Palace.

Richard took seriously his responsibility to support the building work on his cathedral. He encouraged gifts to the fabric fund and directed that certain fines should be granted to it. In his will he left the large sum of forty pounds to the fabric of 'the great church of Chichester'. His most significant contribution was probably to begin the series of chapels along the north and south aisles of the nave. The first was the chapel of St Edmund, where Richard was to be buried.

After Richard was canonized in 1262 and his body moved to the shrine in the retrochoir in 1276, further rebuilding was done, no doubt aided by the increased income from pilgrims to the shrine. The work included the raising of the high roofs of the whole church and, most notably, the extension of the Lady Chapel to its present size.

Above: The chapel in the Bishop's Palace, rebuilt after the fire of 1187, and used by St Richard and his successors.

Right: 13th-century wall painting of the Virgin and Child, from the chapel in the Bishop's Palace. The painting probably dates from just before Richard's time as bishop.

THE CRUSADES

By the time Richard was born Jerusalem had been in Muslim hands for ten years. The Christian kingdom of Jerusalem had lasted less than eighty years and the Arab conquest, begun as long ago as 638, pressed hard on the eastern Roman Empire and on pilgrims from the west. The western Church had long abandoned the early Christian opposition to war, and twice already, in 1095 and 1146, popes had called on the princes and knights of the west to fight under the banner of the cross to recover the Holy Land. A third call went out in 1187 and Richard the Lion Heart, who became king in 1189, was among those who responded. The third crusade was the last in which the princes of the west acted in concert, and, although it re-established some of the Christian principalities, it failed to take Jerusalem from the great Saladin.

The fourth, fifth and sixth crusades were launched in the early thirteenth century. In 1229 the Holy Roman Emperor Frederick regained Jerusalem by negotiation, without striking a blow. However, only a strip of land connected the city to the coastal area that was in Christian hands; most of the Holy Land was disputed between Muslim rulers.

In these circumstances western Christians dreamed of retaking Jerusalem and enabling pilgrims to visit all the places where the Son of God had walked. As Maurice Powicke writes 'The recovery of the Holy Land, whether as an ideal, a symbol, or an immediate duty, pervaded the minds of men in the thirteenth century. It was inseparable from the air they breathed' (*Oxford History of England – the Thirteenth Century*).

The dream was kindled still further when in 1244 (the year before Richard became bishop) ten thousand Turkish tribesmen, encouraged by the ruler of Egypt to undermine the power of his fellow Muslim ruler in Syria, rode into Palestine. Six thousand Christian men, women and children were promised safe conduct out of Jerusalem. By mistake or trickery, only three hundred reached safety; the rest were killed as they tried to reach the coast. The tribesmen sacked Jerusalem. They broke into the church of the Holy Sepulchre, setting it on fire after murdering the priests. When they moved on, the whole city was left desolate.

Pope Innocent IV launched the seventh crusade, appealing both for funds and for Christian princes and knights to fight God's battle and take back the Holy Land. Spiritual blessings were promised to all who committed themselves to this enterprise. Like those who had responded to earlier calls, each was to 'take the cross' – to wear a cross of red material sewed onto his surcoat. It was from this cross (in Latin *crux*) that the soldiers came to be called crusaders. The pope commissioned church leaders to 'preach the Cross' – a blending of devotion to the crucified Jesus with fundraising for the military expedition.

On 6 March 1250 King Henry III himself took the cross, and from then until his death Richard was increasingly involved in the crusade. In October 1250 the pope made him one of the two collectors of funds in England, and in November 1252 the royal council put him in charge of preaching the crusade throughout England. By this time King Louis IX of France had been on crusade for four years, but he was to return home leaving Jerusalem in Muslim hands. Henry III of England stayed at home, having gained a delaying dispensation from the pope.

RICHARD'S LAST JOURNEY

In the spring of 1253 Richard set out to fulfil his commission from the pope and the king to preach the crusade in Sussex and Kent, calling on people to 'take the cross' or give money. He was a man of his time. He would have shared the view of most of his contemporaries that Jerusalem and the Holy Land should be regained for Christendom, accepting that force might be used for this good purpose. However, in describing Richard's journey, Friar Ralph lays more stress on his desire to preach the cross to all than on recruiting and fundraising:

> He set out from his church at Chichester and passing through the towns along the coast and the city of Canterbury ... He worked untiringly in the field of the Lord, furrowing weary hearts with the plough of the cross and the ploughshare of his tongue. He rejoiced to see the fruits of justice spring from the seed of God's word watered by the dew of heavenly grace. Who will be able adequately to describe how he soothed the contrite, heard and instructed those making confession, absolved the penitent, counselled those seeking advice, brought cheer to those in despair, strengthened the fervent, encouraged the timid, and indeed became 'all things to all men'? For he wanted to win all men for Christ and therefore strove to make himself bend to all 'men on account of Christ'. (*Life*, Book 1, section 48)

At the end of his preaching tour Richard reached Dover, and stayed at the Maison Dieu. A chapel had just been completed in the cemetery for the burial of the poor; Richard was invited to dedicate it to St Edmund. Ralph quotes from his sermon on the day of the dedication:

> 'My dearest children, I beg you to join me in blessing God and in praising him who in his grace has permitted us to be present at this dedication in his honour and that of our father, the Blessed Edmund. That is what I have always desired and sought in my prayers ever since I was consecrated as bishop, that before I die I might consecrate at least one church in his honour. Therefore, I thank God from the bottom of my heart, for he has not deprived me of my heart's desire. And now, dearest children, I know that the "laying away of my tabernacle is at hand" [2 Peter 1: 14] and I therefore beg that I may be strengthened and supported by your prayers.'
>
> When the mass had been concluded with due ceremony and he had strengthened the people with his holy blessing the bishop returned to Maison Dieu.

Richard's reference to the laying away of the tabernacle of his body makes it clear that he knew he was soon to die. He even warned one of his priests not to go away to visit his own church: 'If you leave now, before you return the hour will come when you would not be separated from me for the whole Church'.

CHRISTIANS AND NON-CHRISTIANS

Many modern Christians are embarrassed by the crusades. The motives of those who took the cross and set out to re-conquer Jerusalem were as mixed as human motives always are. Ambition, greed and a longing for excitement played their part alongside genuine faith and the desire to walk and pray in the holy places. However, we should not underestimate that faith and devotion.

The actual conduct of many crusaders fell far short of what we would expect of those who wore the cross. When Jerusalem was recaptured in 1095 almost all the Muslim and Jewish inhabitants were butchered. In 1204, seven years after Richard's birth, the army that set out to recapture Jerusalem turned aside and took Constantinople – murdering fellow Christians and looting the city. It took a rare spirit like Francis of Assisi to fight the battle of the cross, not with sword and spear, but with the words of the gospel and a Christlike life.

After the sacking of Jerusalem by Turkish tribesmen in 1244 it would be nearly seven hundred years before a western army again marched into the city. At the time, however, with seemingly endless fighting between rival Muslim rulers, Christians hoped that they might soon regain the city and land where Jesus lived, died and was raised again.

Perhaps even more offensive to us than Richard's support of the crusade is his attitude, shared with his contemporaries, towards the Jews. In his statutes (no. 71) he ordered: 'Jews should be compelled to observe the provisions of the general and special council that they should build no new synagogues and that they should wear a prominent badge to distinguish them from other men. We forbid any Christian man or woman to live with them'. Friar Ralph records with approval that Richard refused a great sum of money offered on behalf of a new synagogue which the Jews had built, rejecting their requests and bribes and not resting until it had been pulled down and demolished (*Life*, Book 1, section 26). He also tells us that Richard solemnly baptised a Jew whom he had instructed in the Christian faith and who wished to receive the grace of baptism; and with the king's permission he gave him the name of the king and willingly adopted him as his own son (*Life*, Book 1, section 39).

Today we must acknowledge that his attitude to the Jews (and even more the attitude of his biographer) is part of a long history of Christian hostility to the people God chose as his own. To them, as St Paul says, 'belong the sonship, the glory, the covenants, the giving of the law, the worship and the promises; to them belong the patriarchs, and of their race, according to the flesh, is the Christ' (Romans 9: 4, 5). Yet Christians have, until very recently, condemned them as the murderers of Jesus, and this has provided a justification for acts of unspeakable evil. Christians today have begun to recognize a duty to change such attitudes – not by feeling guilty for things that happened long ago, but in the New Testament sense of a change of heart, by seeking ways of understanding and being reconciled with those of different faiths and religious practices.

Among those who are being persecuted for their faith today are many Christians. To them the only adequate words are those of Jesus: 'blessed are those who are persecuted for righteousness' sake, for theirs is the kingdom of heaven' (Matthew 5: 10).

RICHARD'S DEATH

Richard had rightly foreseen his own death. He had consecrated the new chapel on Sunday 30 March 1253. The next day he went to the chapel of the Maison Dieu and collapsed during morning prayer. Friar Ralph describes how the attendants lifted Richard up and carried him to his bed. His illness grew worse each day, and he knew that the time had come when he would 'be summoned from the world'.

Richard made a general confession, received the sacraments, and told his closest attendants to make preparations for his funeral. Friar Ralph writes movingly of the events that followed:

> Father Simon said 'My lord, the season of our Lord's passion is nigh, and as you have shared his sorrows, you will share his consolation'. At this the holy man seemed to grow more cheerful … [and] said 'Not tomorrow, but the following Friday I shall enjoy a great feast'. The day and hour of his death afterwards proved this to be true … He was now very weak … He embraced the image of the Crucified, which he had asked to be brought to him … He devoutly kissed and tenderly caressed the wounds as if he had just seen them newly inflicted on his Saviour's dying body, and cried out, 'I thank thee, my Lord Jesus Christ, for all the benefits which thou hast granted to me, for all the pains and insults which thou hast suffered for me'.
>
> He said to his attendants, 'Place this wretched body down on the ground'. For, as he had known in his lifetime to chastise the limbs of his naturally handsome body … so when dying did he know how to humble it still more with his humility. Often repeating the words of the psalmist, 'Into thy hands, O Lord, I commend my spirit', and then turning with both heart and voice to the glorious Virgin, he said 'Mary, mother of grace, mother of mercy, protect us from the Enemy now, and pray for us at the hour of our death'. Thus … the blessed Richard rendered up his soul, soon to join those that dwell in the kingdom above, to his Creator.
>
> He passed from this world in about the fifty-sixth year of his age, in the ninth year of his episcopate, on April 3rd, at about midnight, when it is said that the heavenly Bridegroom will come to the nuptials, to enjoy with the Bride the pleasures of the heavenly court, by the mercy of him who with the Father and the Holy Spirit lives and reigns as God for ever and ever (*Life*, Book 1 section 48).

Panel depicting the death of Richard, from a series embroidered for Chichester Cathedral in 1975 to commemorate the 900th anniversary of the Cathedral. Designed by Yvonne Hudson and Rosalie Williams.

RICHARD'S BURIAL

Richard's body was, as he had required in his will, taken back to Chichester Cathedral for burial, while his heart and other organs were interred in the chapel he had just dedicated to St Edmund.

When they washed him they found that, although he had mortified his body by wearing a hair shirt and various knots and belts, it 'shone with such a radiant whiteness that, although dead, it seemed to offer some portent of future resurrection'.

Friar Ralph describes the funeral procession:

> So his body was carried to Chichester and as it passed by monasteries, churches, towns or villages, the bells rang and the cortege was greeted with solemn psalms and tears, for although the people knew that they had lost the bodily presence of so great a pastor, they hoped that they would be protected by his heavenly patronage and intervention and regarded themselves as fortunate if so great a treasure rested with them for a single night.
>
> When, therefore, they reached the city which was honoured to have been the seat of his diocese, rich and poor alike rushed eagerly from the streets and alleyways, the rich mourning and weeping on account of the honour he had done them, the poor because of the great amount of alms that he had given them while living ... So they carried the body into the cathedral and you would have heard music mix not inappropriately with the sounds of grief ... His venerable body was buried in a humble place in that same church, near the altar of the Blessed Edmund the Confessor which he himself had built on the northern side of the cathedral, where great and wonderful miracles were performed (*Life*, Book 1, section 49)

Restored altar in St Edmund's Chapel in Dover. Under the right of the altar is the cavity in which St Richard's heart was probably buried.

Opposite: The chapel of St Edmund of Abingdon and St Thomas Becket, on the north side of Chichester Cathedral. Richard had this chapel built and, as requested in his will, he was buried here in 1253.

O ye priests of the Lord bless ye the Lord

THE CANONIZATION OF SAINT RICHARD

In 1256, three years after Richard's death, the bishop and canons of Chichester, supported by King Henry III as well as many bishops and nobles, petitioned the pope to enquire into Richard's life and miracles. A commission of three was appointed, comprising the Bishop of Hereford, the provincial prior of the English Dominicans, and a Franciscan friar. They had collected evidence and reported to the pope by May 1261.

Their evidence was examined by officials of the papal curia, led by Bishop Odo of Tusculum. One of his surviving sermons includes material submitted to the pope in support of Richard's canonization. Eventually, in Friar Ralph's words: 'the Holy Father, attended by the cardinals and a great throng of both clergy and people, on St Vincent's day [22 January 1262], at the church of the Friars Minor in Viterbo, most devoutly and solemnly placed him in the ranks of the saints. And the Lord Pope himself pronounced the sentence of canonization amid tears of joy and everyone gave thanks to God who had made St Richard the like of the saints in glory'.

The iron screen that formerly surrounded Richard's shrine in Chichester Cathedral is now part of the gates to the Lady Chapel.

The letter of canonization was sent out a month later. In it the pope, borrowing words from the Easter liturgy, writes:

> Let the angelic host of heaven now exult, let the divine mysteries exult ... let the saints exult in glory ... let Mother Church exult' ... let England exult ... let the church of Chichester exult and rejoice that she has deserved so great a pastor, who in his lifetime taught her with counsels of salvation, instructed her with praiseworthy examples and after his death fortified her with the goodwill of men and protected her with his intercession before God.

The pope concluded his letter by encouraging pilgrimages to St Richard's shrine and ordering that 'each year on April 3rd you will solemnly celebrate his feast', using proper prayers which 'he had himself composed and chanted'.

THE SHRINE OF SAINT RICHARD

Fourteen years after his canonization and twenty-six years after his death, the body of St Richard was moved – the technical term is *translated* – to a shrine behind the high altar of Chichester Cathedral. His head was enshrined separately in the chapel of St Mary Magdalene, where its niche can still be seen. There were now three places of prayer in the Cathedral to which pilgrims came – the original burial place in the chapel of St Edmund and St Thomas; the silver-gilt, jewel-encrusted shrine in the retrochoir; and the silver reliquary of the head.

SYMBOLS AND BADGES

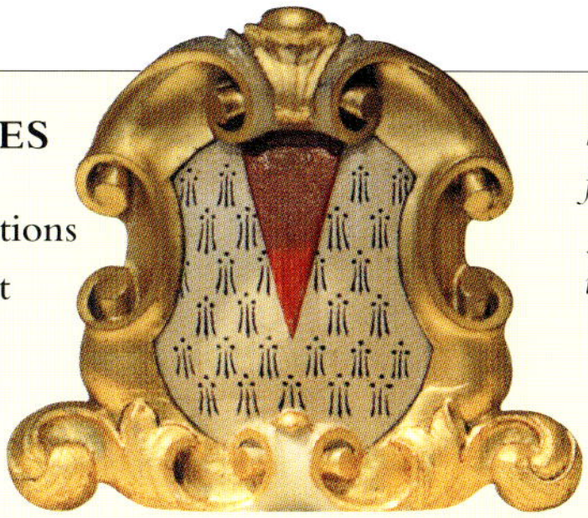

St Richard's second and less frequently seen coat of arms, from the chapel of St Richard in St Andrew's, Worthing.

Medieval representations of saints were not intended to be portraits, so one holy bishop would look like another. To distinguish them the practice grew up of putting different symbols in their hands or at their feet. In England the saints were often given heraldic coats of arms as well – even when, like St Richard, they lived before heraldry was fully established.

St Richard has been given two separate coats of arms. The more common shows a cross with a cup in each quarter of the shield. Sometimes the cups are covered, and sometimes they are open and contain wine. This may refer to the miracle of the overturned cup, often shown in modern statues of St Richard (see page 13). The story – not found in the ancient sources – tells that Richard, tired and ill from his labours, was celebrating mass and dropped the chalice containing the consecrated wine. Miraculously, none of the sacramental Blood of Christ was spilled.

The heraldic shield of the bishops of Chichester is based on the visions in the last book of the Bible (*Revelation* 1:13 to 16, combined with 20:12). The glorified Christ is shown sitting on a throne, holding the book of life, and with a sharp two-edged sword coming out of his mouth.

Heraldic shields embroidered on a cope belonging to St Andrew's, Worthing. Left: shield of St Richard; right: shield of the bishops of Chichester.

Niche in the chapel of St Mary Magdalene, Chichester Cathedral, where St Richard's head was enshrined.

Pilgrims came to pray particularly on 3 April (the *dies natalis*, or heavenly birthday), and on the 'Feast of Translation' on 16 June. The annual payments from parishes to the cathedral came to be known as 'St Richard's Pence'. They and other gifts enriched the shrine for the next two hundred and fifty years.

Richard did not become a particularly popular saint outside his own diocese. Apparently only one mediaeval church was dedicated in his honour, but relics were taken to Canterbury and also to several churches in Normandy. At Droitwich, St Richard's Well was a focus of popular devotion, continuing even after it had been forbidden under the Puritans. We cannot know how many representations of St Richard there were in England, but wall paintings survive in Norwich Cathedral and in the parish church of Black Bourton.

Despite the inclusion of Henry VIII as a benefactor in the sixteenth-century painting by Lambert Barnard in Chichester Cathedral's south transept, St Richard's shrine shared the fate of almost all the shrines in England under this king. On 20 November 1538 the royal commissioners carried out their instructions to destroy the shine, raising it to

Left: 13th-century wall painting of St Richard in the parish church of Black Bourton, Oxfordshire.

Above: Line drawing based on the wall painting at Black Bourton.

Above: 14th-century wall painting in Norwich Cathedral, showing Richard with his mitre and crozier. Despite the deterioration, these can still be identified at the top and on the right.

the ground and taking away coffers, caskets, and a small box containing gold, silver, jewels, relics and ornaments. The only surviving elements of the shrine seem to be parts of the surrounding iron screen now incorporated in the gates to the Lady Chapel. There is no record of the fate of Richard's body or head.

SAINT RICHARD REDISCOVERED

The nineteenth century saw a renewal of interest in the history, art and devotion of the Middle Ages. As with other medieval saints, depictions of St Richard began to appear in stained glass windows (see page 2), and in 1894 a statue was placed in St Richard's Porch, the south porch of Chichester Cathedral.

The Chichester Cathedral banner. St Richard is shown with St Wilfrid, the first bishop in Sussex. Designed by Ernest Geldard and made by Miss Harvey, c.1900.

Opposite: St Richard's Porch on the south of Chichester Cathedral. The statue of Richard is by Harry Hems, 1894.

Inset top: Procession to the shrine at the conclusion of The Acts of Saint Richard, *performed at Chichester Cathedral in 1953, the 700th anniversary year.*

Inset bottom: Bishop Eric Kemp dedicating the altar at the shrine of St Richard, Chichester Cathedral, June 1984.

At the turn of the twentieth century the 'Prayer of St Richard' was published (see back cover). Although only its first two lines can be attributed to St Richard – they appear in Friar Ralph's account of his death – its devotion to Jesus as Redeemer, Friend and Brother is faithful to Richard's own spirituality. Much later in the century, the prayer gained wider circulation by its use in the musical *Godspell*.

In 1930 an altar was placed on the site of the shrine in Chichester Cathedral. This altar became the focus of regular pilgrimages, including a solemn procession on the 'Feast of the Translation'. As 3 April often falls in Holy Week or Easter Week, the 16 June is kept as the principal feast in the diocese. The annual festival of the Friends of the Cathedral takes place on this day too.

Bishop George Bell was Bishop of Chichester at the time of the 700th anniversary of St Richard's death, in 1953, and he issued a spiritual call 'to every priest and every parish in the diocese to renew their discipleship, and to pray to God for a fresh outpouring of the Holy Spirit'. During the year the bishops visited each deanery, and in Chichester there were lectures and special services, including a celebration of the Eucharist by the Archbishop of Canterbury. There was also a pageant in which *The Acts of Saint Richard* were performed in the palace forecourt. Each performance ended with a procession of clergy, actors and audience to the shrine. Bishop Bell also created a Guild of St Richard for the newly confirmed.

Since 1953 the shrine of St Richard has been further enriched. The 'Anglo-German Tapestry', which includes references to the saint's life, was commissioned to mark the centenary of Bishop Bell's birth in 1983. Seven years later, a portion of an authenticated relic of St Richard was given to the shrine. This fragment of bone, probably of St Richard's arm, had been preserved at the abbey of La Lucerne in Normandy from soon after 1276, and had recently been traced and identified by the restorer of the abbey, the Abbé Marcel Lelégard. The relic was interred beneath the altar of the shrine on St Richard's day, 1991. Here pilgrims are invited to light candles and to leave requests for prayer. These requests are offered at the altar during the Cathedral Eucharist every day. Since the summer of 2002 the Eucharist has been celebrated at the shrine at noon each Saturday.

Below: The abbey of La Lucerne, Normandy.

Opposite: The altar of St Richard and the 'Anglo-German Tapestry', installed in June 1985. Interred under the altar is the relic of St Richard from the arm preserved in the abbey of La Lucerne.

On 16 June 2002 Bishop John Hind called the diocese of Chichester to mark the 750th anniversary of St Richard's death by 'finding simple ways to know Jesus more clearly, love Jesus more dearly and follow Jesus more nearly'. He also announced that the celebrations of the 'Year of Saint Richard' would include a pilgrimage through the diocese, starting on 3 April 2003 at St Edmund's chapel in Dover and passing through all twenty-one deaneries, culminating in a diocesan festival at Chichester Cathedral in June, near the anniversary of the translation in 1276. An icon was commissioned to be carried in this pilgrimage.

So it is that people from all over Sussex and beyond come again to pray in this place made holy by the presence and prayers of St Richard. Pilgrims come from many congregations, including the Roman Catholic parish of St Richard in Chichester, which celebrates a mass on the feast each year. In the diocese of Chichester there are at present ten churches dedicated to St Richard, and the city's hospital in Spitalfield Lane also bears his name. His memory does not fade in the county he served as teacher, pastor and reformer.

A SAINT FOR US

Statue of St Richard outside the cathedral. He is holding a scourge, the symbol of his self-discipline and his identification with the sufferings of Jesus.

Much of what we know about St Richard will seem strange to us. We are, after all, commemorating a man who died 750 years ago. His world was different from ours, and his way of being a Christian was different from ours.

We need not hesitate to say that some of Richard's views and actions were wrong, but that does not mean that we should refuse to acknowledge him as a saint. To do that would lead us to deny the title to any of the disciples of Jesus. A saint is not someone who makes no mistakes, but a follower of the crucified and risen Lord, through whose weaknesses and strengths he reveals himself to others. That is what he did through Richard. In him we can recognize the authentic marks of one who has 'been with Jesus' (Acts 4: 3). So our thanksgiving can go hand in hand with our penitence as we in our day seek to *'follow Jesus more nearly'*.

ENGLAND FROM 1197 TO 1253

When Richard was born in 1197, Richard I (The Lion Heart) had two more years to live. He spent all but six months of his ten-year reign outside England, defending his other lands from the king of France, and fighting unsuccessfully to recapture Jerusalem. He had left the government of England in the hands of royal officers and his brother John. There had been a continuous struggle for power between them, and the struggle continued when John succeeded his brother as king.

Richard grew up during the troubled times of King John. The years 1199–1216 saw war between king and barons and the signing of Magna Carta. In 1204 Normandy (except for the Channel Islands) was lost to the English crown. For six years the whole realm was under an interdict which meant that churches were closed and the sacraments could not be celebrated. Eventually John himself was excommunicated. By this time at least ten of the seventeen dioceses were either vacant or had their bishops in exile. The interdict was lifted only when John resigned his kingdom to the pope and received it back as a papal vassal. When John died in 1216 half of England was held by a French army and rebel barons. The heir was John's nine-year-old son, who was proclaimed king as Henry III.

This unpromising start to the new reign was steadily reversed. The royal council, and then the king himself from 1227 when he reached the age of 19, defeated the French army and regained control of the kingdom. However, the country's troubles were not over. Like his father, Henry was often in conflict with the barons, the bishops and the pope. Among the causes of conflict was his concern with the other lands of his empire (Normandy, Anjou and Poitou) as well as the influence of his wife's relatives, who were thought to encourage his overseas claims. There were brief periods of civil war, which would culminate in the king's defeat by Simon de Monfort at the battle of Lewes in 1264. Despite this tension, England was increasingly prosperous during Henry's reign.

Like his his grandfather, King Henry II, and his father, King John, Henry III was a man of violent and changing passions. He was genuinely devout and often generous to churches, but that did not stop him opposing the wishes of churchmen. His changeable attitude is seen in the fact that, having opposed the appointment of Richard as bishop, and continuing to withhold the income of the bishopric right up to his death, he was nevertheless among those who petitioned the pope for Richard's canonization.

Henry's patronage of the arts and the church shows most clearly in the rebuilding of Edward the Confessor's abbey of Westminster.

Bronze tomb effigy of Henry III in Westminster Abbey. Made by London goldsmith William Torel, 1292.